Play
Chess
in 10

minutes

Brian Byfield

Illustrations by Gray Jolliffe

BATSFORD

First published in the United Kingdom in 2011 by
Batsford, 10 Southcombe Street, London W14 0RA

An imprint of Anova Books Company Ltd

ISBN 978 1 84994 015 3

A CIP catalogue record for this book is available from the
British Library.

18 17 16 15 14 13 12 11
10 9 8 7 6 5 4 3 2 1

Reproduction by Dot Gradations, UK
Printed and bound by Toppan Leefung Printing Ltd, China

Cartoons hand coloured, using
the TRIA system by LETRASET

www.letraset.com

Chess is the most popular board game in the world. Maybe because it's a war game. But unlike in a real war, you don't have to win the hearts and minds of the people, you just wipe them out.

Most people think Chess is a difficult game to learn. In fact, it really is quite easy.

Right, we haven't got much time, so let's start.

There are 32 pieces, 16 black and 16 white. When you start a game the board should look like this:

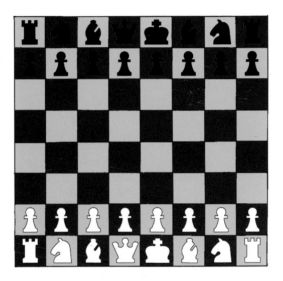

Make sure you get a light square in the bottom right-hand corner.

The white Queen always goes on a light square and the black Queen on a dark square.

It all looks very complicated. But don't worry.
You only have to learn how to move six of them:

the Pawn

the Knight

the Bishop

the Rook

the Queen

the King

Once you know how they move and capture,
you're on your way.

PUSHY PAWNS

He's the brave little foot soldier who marches into battle and cannot move backwards. Here's how he moves:

He can only move one square at a time in a straight line. Except for his first move, where he can move two squares.

Of course, if there's a piece on the square in front of him, he can't move. When he captures an enemy piece, he moves one square diagonally. So that's the Pawn: you have eight of them. And now you know how to move them all.

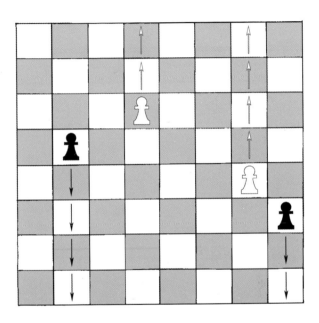

Pawns move one square at a time.

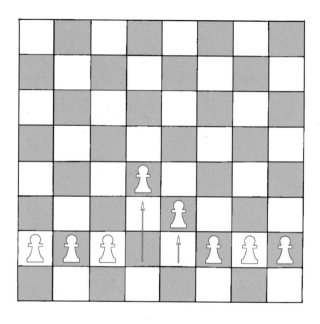

On your first move you can move one or
two squares.

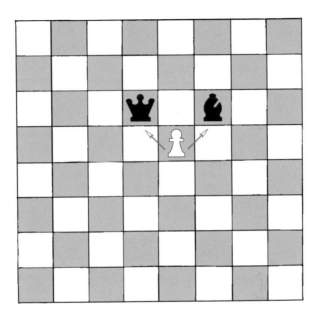

The Pawn can take the Queen or the Bishop.

When you capture an enemy piece, it's taken off the board, and the capturing piece occupies its square.

If a brave Pawn makes it across to the other side of the board, it can move no further and must become a Queen, or any other piece of his choice, except a King.

There is another Pawn move called 'En Passant'. But there's no time to tell you about that.

NAUGHTY KNIGHTS

Basically, the Knight is a man on a horse, so he can jump over enemy pieces. This is how he moves:

Two squares straight and one square to the side, **or** one square straight and two squares to the side.

As you can see, it's an L shape. He captures enemy pieces exactly the same way, taking the piece on the square he lands on. The Knight is the only piece that can jump over other pieces, friend or foe. You have two Knights on your board.

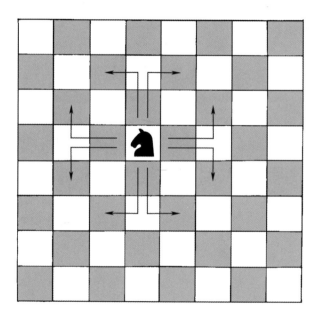

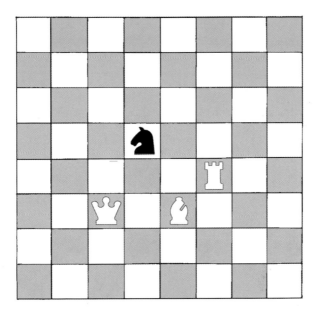

The Knight can take the Queen, the Bishop or
the Rook.

BRUTAL BISHOPS

The Bishop is really a thug in a clerical robe.

He moves along the diagonals to anywhere on the board, and can capture any piece of his opponent in his path. In your army, you've got two Bishops. One stays on the white and the other on the black squares.

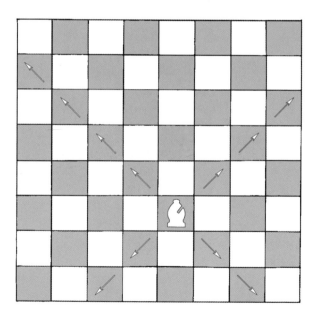

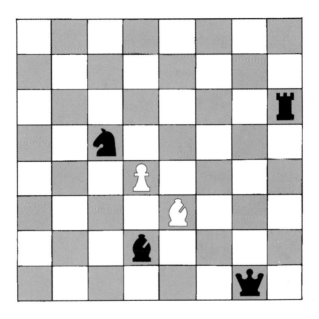

The White Bishop can't take the Knight because his Pawn is in the way. He can capture the Queen, Rook or Bishop.

RUTHLESS ROOKS

He's more commonly known by his nom de guerre, the Rook. He can move on any straight line along the Ranks and Files. He can't move diagonally.

We call him 'Rook'

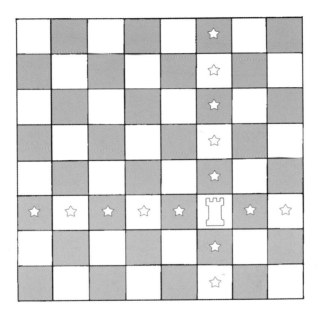

So he can move one square at a time or in one
long, sweeping move.

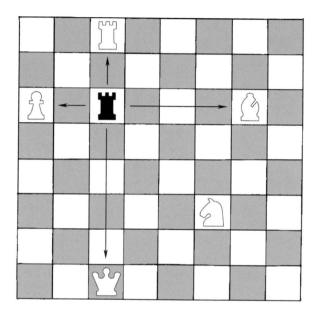

The only piece the Black Rook can't take is the Knight, because he's on a diagonal.

You have two Rooks and they're a deadly team. Between them they can cover 28 squares. That's nearly half of the board. When you've got two of your opponent's Rooks on your tail, don't let your King anywhere near them.

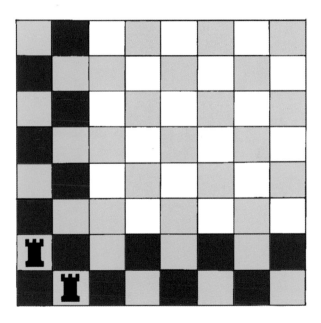

KILLER
QUEENS

The Queen is a rough, tough, fighting machine;
Attila the Hun in drag. She can move anywhere
on ranks, files and diagonals. But she can't jump
over other pieces and she can't turn corners in a
single move like a Knight. Nevertheless, she's the
most powerful piece in your army.

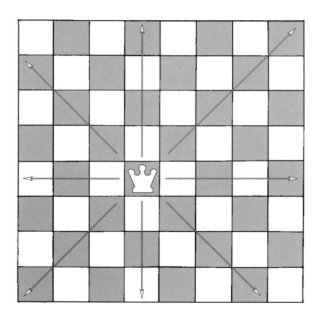

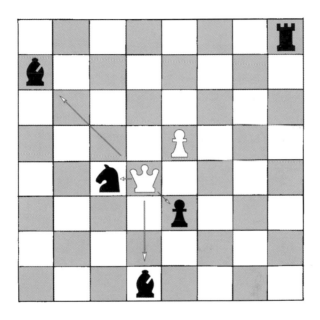

The Queen's Pawn stops her from capturing the Black Rook.

KLUTZY
KINGS

The King is the most important piece on the board. Your job is to protect him. And boy, does he need it.

He is slow and lazy, and will expect his army to do the dirty work. He can only move one square at a time in any direction.

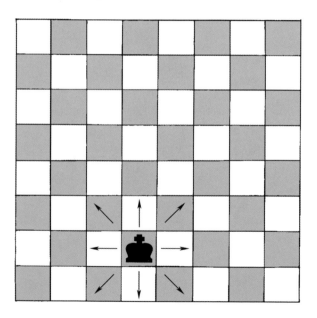

He captures enemy pieces in the same way.

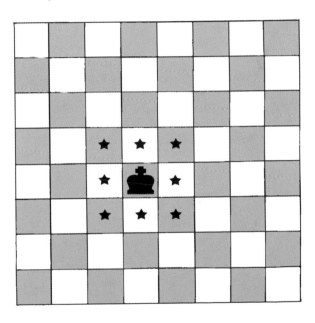

Your King is allowed to Castle during a game, which means you make two moves at once, repositioning your King and your Rook in one go. But remember: you can't Castle to get out of Check, or if Castling lands the King in a Check, or if in the process of Castling the King jumps over a square that would be Check. Nor can you Castle if the King or the Rook have already moved or if there's another piece in the way. Castling helps you to get your King into a safer position and your Rook out of the corner into the action. See page 45 if you want to know what 'Check' means.

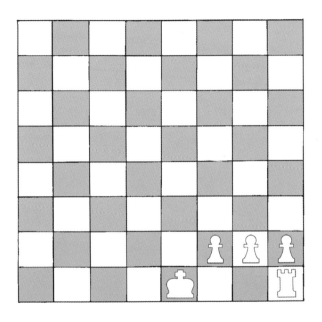

The King is ready to Castle on the King side.

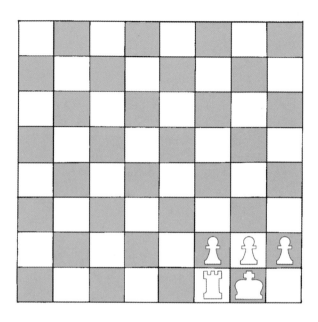

This is what it looks like when he has.

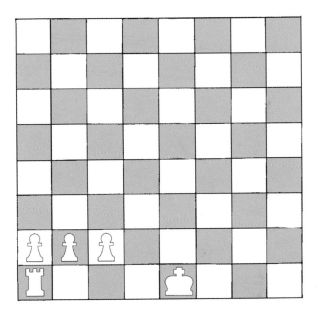

The King is ready to Castle on the Queen side.

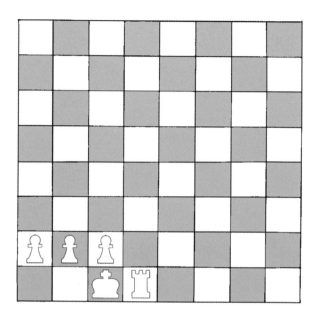

This is what it looks like when he has.

The objective of the game is to trap the King. You do this by putting him in Check, which is when he is threatened with capture by one or more of the enemy pieces.

When the King is in a position where he cannot move or defend himself, he loses the game. This is called Checkmate.

Ok, your 10 minutes are up. You should now be ready to play.

The great thing is that by learning how to move six pieces, you can now move all 32.

Set up your board and find someone to play with.

Remember, the white Queen goes on the light squares and the black Queen on the dark squares. White always goes first.

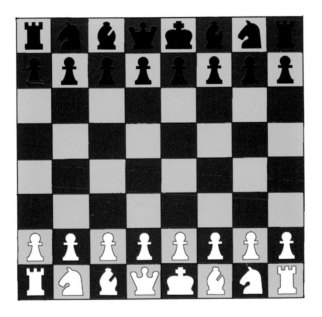

Although you now know how to play Chess, you'll still need to learn a lot more to play well. Here are some tips that might help.

As a general rule, start with your Pawns, then your Knights and Bishops, and then your Rooks and Queen.

Usually a game is won or lost by the quality of the positions of your pieces on the board. And controlling the centre, just like in a boxing ring or a squash court, gives your pieces more mobility. Try not to get them stuck at the side of the board; it gives you fewer options for your moves. Control the centre and you control the game.

When you play, try to remember that an army marches on its stomach. So make sure you have support when you make an attack.

Don't get greedy and go rushing around the board picking off Pawns with your Queen. She could get cut off from her troops and face a lingering death.

Also, try to move forward carefully and avoid having to move backwards.

If you see a Chess problem or game in a
newspaper or magazine, the moves are recorded
by a system called 'algebraic notation'. There's
no time to go into details, but it's a little like
Battleships. Here's how it works.

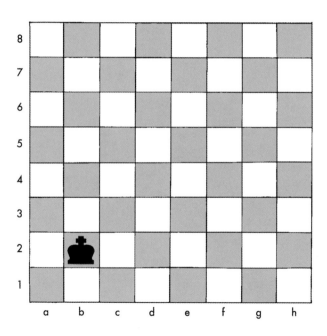

So the King is on b2. That's it. Get the picture?

By the way,

means a piece is taken,

means Check, and

means Checkmate.

These are the letters and symbols used for the pieces.

KING	K	
QUEEN	Q	
ROOK	R	
BISHOP	B	
KNIGHT	N	
PAWN	P	

This is how you judge the value of the pieces:

The Queen   –   9 points
The Rook   –   5 points
The Knight –   3 points
The Bishop –   3 points
The Pawn   –   1 point

The King, although of little value as a fighting force, is the most important piece of all. He must be defended at all costs. If he goes, the game's up.

This gives you an idea of what each piece is worth. It's only a rough guide, but think about it when you lose your Queen to capture a Pawn.

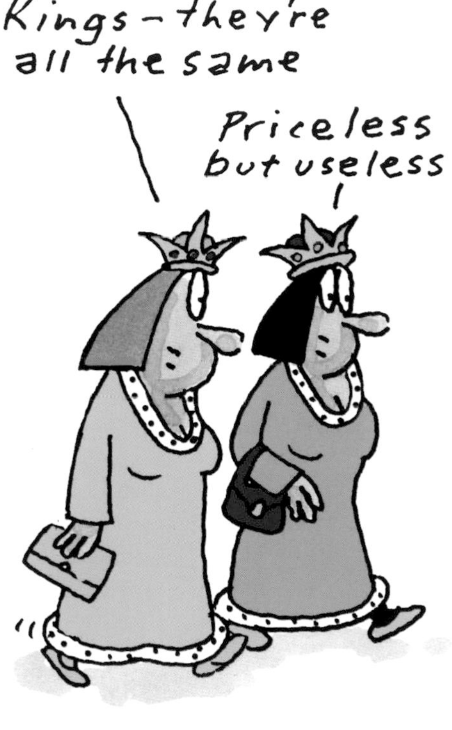
Kings – they're all the same
Priceless but useless

As this is a very short book, here's a very short game. In fact, it's the shortest game that can be played in Chess. It's called Fool's Mate. And this is what happens. Hopefully you will be playing Black.

White to move   Black

1.	f3	e5
2.	g4	Qh4!
		# Checkmate

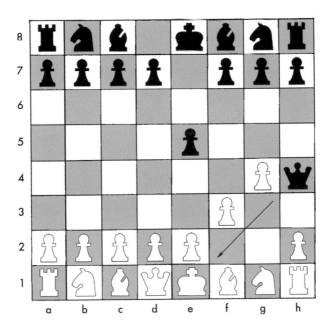

Of course, there are still lots of things to learn. En Passant, Forks, Pins, Skewers, Double Checks, Double Attacks and Sacrifices. You'll pick them up as you go along.

And, remember, your job is to manoeuvre your pieces to victory by capturing the enemy King, or winning so many of your opponent's pieces that he gives up the fight and 'resigns'.

Keep your eyes on every one of the 64 squares of the battlefield.

Try to see every threat as an opportunity, and every opportunity as a potential minefield.

Officially, there is no such thing as luck in Chess. So if you lose you've only got yourself to blame.

And, by the way, if you want to improve and learn more, you'll have to buy a bigger book than this one.

After all, there's only so much you can learn in 10 minutes.

Moving on

Your first win will always be a special moment, but losing at Chess is not the end of the world. Playing with better players is the best way to improve. You will learn a lot just by watching how they manoeuvre their pieces. So even if you feel powerless to stop their advance, you'll be able to appreciate the way they organise their pieces into a deadly attack.

If you can't find time to play, there is a Chess column in most newspapers. They usually explain a game and how it was played out. You will also find a problem to solve. Solving Chess problems is a great way to practise and keep your brain cells working. Don't worry if at first you have to look up the answer. The answer will also explain why the key move is more effective than any other move.

Working out the best possible move is the secret to winning Chess. But remember, working out your opponent's best move is equally important. And all the more satisfying if you know what it is and your opponent doesn't.

Whatever happens, have fun, don't feel too smug if you win – at least, try not to show it – and if you do keep losing, the good news is you'll always find someone to play with.